Delivery Trucks

by Adele D. Richardson

Consultant:
Bill Johnson
Assistant Managing Director
American Truck Historical Society

Bridgestone Books
an imprint of Capstone Press
Mankato, Minnesota

Bridgestone Books are published by Capstone Press
151 Good Counsel Drive, P.O. Box 669, Mankato, Minnesota 56002
http://www.capstone-press.com

Library of Congress Cataloging-in-Publication Data
Richardson, Adele D., 1966–
    Delivery trucks/by Adele D. Richardson.
    p. cm.—(The transportation library)
    Includes bibliographical references and index.
    Summary: Describes early models, major parts, and the workings of delivery trucks.
    ISBN 0-7368-0609-1
    1. Trucks—Juvenile literature. 2. Delivery of goods—Juvenile literature. [1. Trucks.] I. Title.
II. Series.
TL230.15 .R53 2001
629.224—dc21   00-022827

Editorial Credits
Karen L. Daas, editor; Timothy Halldin, cover designer and illustrator;
    Kimberly Danger and Heidi Schoof, photo researchers

Photo Credits
Archive Photos, 12, 14
FPG International, LLC, 16
Kimberly Danger, cover, 6, 10, 20
Shaffer Photography/James L. Shaffer, 4, 18

1 2 3 4 5 6 06 05 04 03 02 01

Table of Contents

Delivery Trucks

Delivery trucks are vehicles that transport cargo from place to place. Some delivery trucks have racks inside to hold cargo. Delivery trucks are bigger than cars and vans. They are smaller than tractor trailers.

cargo
goods that are carried from one place to another

window

wheel

driver's seat

cargo area

Parts of a Delivery Truck

A delivery truck has a driver's seat. A cargo area is behind the driver's seat. A delivery truck has a large front window. One or two doors are near the front of the delivery truck. A large door is at the back of the delivery truck. A delivery truck has four or six wheels.

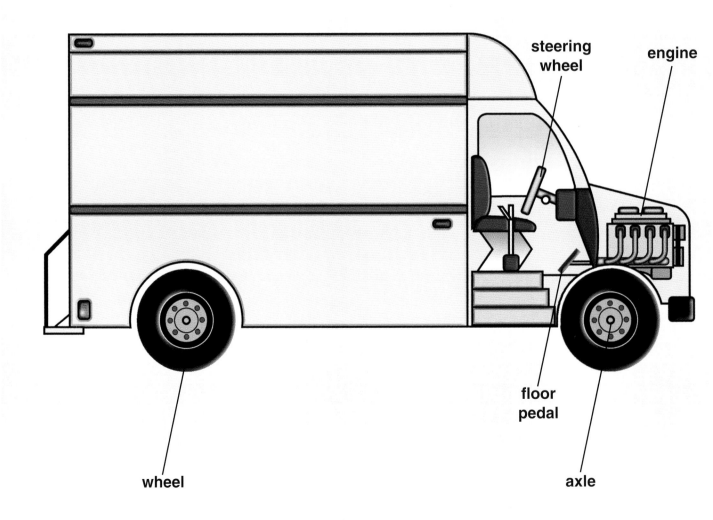

steering
wheel

engine

floor
pedal

wheel

axle

How a Delivery Truck Works

A delivery truck works like a car. Gas powers the engine. The engine's power turns the axles. The axles turn the wheels. A driver uses floor pedals to control the delivery truck's speed. A driver uses the steering wheel to turn the delivery truck.

axle
a rod in the center of a wheel; axles turn wheels.

Driving a Delivery Truck

Delivery truck drivers load goods at a warehouse. Drivers place goods in the cargo area. They then transport the cargo to another place. Drivers make many stops within a city or small area. They keep records of the deliveries they make.

warehouse

a large building used for storing goods

Before Delivery Trucks

Horse-drawn wagons transported cargo before delivery trucks were invented. Businesses needed to hire many people to care for their horses. Horses were not strong enough to pull heavy cargo. They also traveled more slowly than delivery trucks do.

13

Early Delivery Trucks

In the 1890s, companies began to build delivery trucks. Steam and electric engines powered most of these trucks. Many businesses soon began to use delivery trucks instead of horse-drawn wagons. The businesses could deliver goods faster with delivery trucks.

Later Delivery Trucks

In the 1950s, companies built special delivery trucks that looked like vans. The driver could walk into the cargo area from the front of the truck. This new design also allowed more room for cargo inside the delivery truck.

Delivery Trucks Today

Delivery trucks transport food, water, and clothing. They transport games and books. Delivery trucks carry packages and mail. They transport almost everything people buy.

Delivery Truck Facts

- Delivery trucks with refrigerated areas are called reefers. They keep food from spoiling before it is delivered.

- Bottlers are delivery trucks that transport large bottles of water.

- A bookmobile is a type of delivery truck. This moving library carries books from place to place.

- Delivery trucks are different sizes. Delivery trucks can be light trucks or medium trucks. Light trucks weigh less than 10,000 pounds (4,500 kilograms). Medium trucks weigh between 10,000 pounds (4,500 kilograms) and 20,000 pounds (9,000 kilograms).

Hands On: Delivery Routes

Delivery truck drivers deliver cargo to many places each day. They plan their routes to make the most deliveries in the least amount of time. You can plan a delivery route.

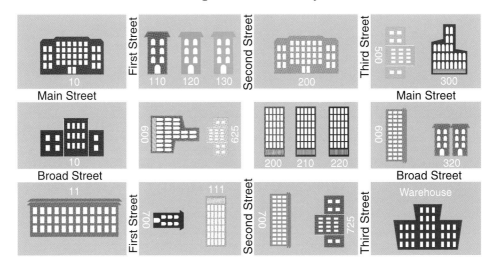

Find the shortest delivery route between the following places:
1. Pick up your cargo at the warehouse.
2. Make deliveries to these locations:
   - 10 Main Street
   - 200 Main Street
   - 600 First Street
   - 625 Second Street
   - 200 Broad Street

Words To Know

axle (AK-suhl)—a rod in the center of a wheel; axles turn wheels.

cargo (KAR-goh)—goods that are carried from one place to another

engine (EN-juhn)—a machine that makes the power needed to move something

transport (transs-PORT)—to move people or goods from one place to another

vehicle (VEE-uh-kuhl)—something that carries people and goods from one place to another

warehouse (WAIR-hous)—a large building used for storing goods

Read More

Gibson, Karen Bush. *Truck Drivers.* Mankato, Minn.: Bridgestone Books, 2001.

McNaught, Harry. *Trucks.* Jellybean Books. New York: Random House, 1998.

Stille, Darlene R. *Trucks.* A True Book. New York: Children's Press, 1997.

Internet Sites

The AA Truck Page
http://www.netclassics.com/truck/aa-truck.html
American Truck Historical Society
http://www.aths.org
Kids Korner
http://www.ontruck.org/kids/index.htm

Index